KEEPING IT
REAL AND RELEVANT

IGNACIO LOPEZ

KEEPING IT
REAL AND RELEVANT

BUILDING AUTHENTIC RELATIONSHIPS
IN YOUR DIVERSE CLASSROOM

Alexandria, Virginia USA

1703 N. Beauregard St. • Alexandria, VA 22311-1714 USA
Phone: 800-933-2723 or 703-578-9600 • Fax: 703-575-5400
Website: www.ascd.org • E-mail: member@ascd.org
Author guidelines: www.ascd.org/write

Deborah S. Delisle, *Executive Director;* Robert D. Clouse, *Managing Director, Digital Content & Publications;* Stefani Roth, *Publisher;* Genny Ostertag, *Director, Content Acquisitions;* Julie Houtz, *Director, Book Editing & Production;* Joy Scott Ressler, *Editor;* Georgia Park, *Senior Graphic Designer;* Mike Kalyan, *Director, Production Services;* Michael Podgorny, *Production Specialist;* Circle Graphics, Inc., *Typesetter.*

All web links in this book are correct as of the publication date below but may have become inactive or otherwise modified since that time. If you notice a deactivated or changed link, please e-mail books@ascd.org with the words "Link Update" in the subject line. In your message, please specify the web link, the book title, and the page number on which the link appears.

PAPERBACK ISBN: 978-1-4166-2440-0   ASCD product #117049   n8/17
PDF E-BOOK ISBN: 978-1-4166-2442-4; see Books in Print for other formats.

Quantity discounts are available: e-mail programteam@ascd.org or call 800-933-2723, ext. 5773, or 703-575-5773. For desk copies, go to www.ascd.org/deskcopy.

Library of Congress Cataloging-in-Publication Data

Names: Lopez, Ignacio, 1979- author.
Title: Keeping it real and relevant : building authentic relationships in your diverse classroom / Ignacio Lopez.
Description: Alexandria, Virginia, USA : ASCD, [2017] | Includes bibliographical references and index.
Identifiers: LCCN 2017022877 (print) | LCCN 2017029905 (ebook) | ISBN 9781416624424 (PDF) | ISBN 9781416624400 (pbk.)
Subjects: LCSH: Culturally relevant pedagogy. | Teacher-student relationships.
Classification: LCC LB1033 (ebook) | LCC LB1033 .L66 2017 (print) | DDC 370.117–dc23
LC record available at https://lccn.loc.gov/2017022877

25 24 23 22 21 20 19 18 17   1 2 3 4 5 6 7 8 9 10 11 12

For my wife and kids,
who always help me
Keep It Real.

KEEPING IT
REAL AND RELEVANT

BUILDING AUTHENTIC RELATIONSHIPS IN YOUR DIVERSE CLASSROOM

Preface ix

Introduction xi

Chapter 1: Self-Awareness: Relationship-Building
in Diverse Classrooms 1

Chapter 2: Designing and Leveraging an Effective
Learning Environment 11

Chapter 3: Reality Therapy in Diverse Classrooms 19

Chapter 4: Nonpunitive Interventions in Diverse Classrooms 29

Chapter 5: The Making of an Expert 43

Chapter 6: Work Ethic in Diverse Classrooms 55

Chapter 7: Characteristics of Successful Teachers
in Diverse Classrooms 67

Bibliography 73

Index 77

About the Author 81

Preface

This book is the result of my journey as a classroom teacher, school leader, instructional coach, and researcher. When I first began teaching, I assumed that because I looked and sounded like many of my students, we would be able to build strong relationships with one another. I was wrong: my students saw me as more foreign than I could have imagined. I remember needing to step back from curriculum planning for a bit to consider how I might build their trust and confidence in me as their teacher. I set out to read up on, discover, and try new approaches intended to hook my students, many of whom were new to this country, on learning.

I remember attending several professional development workshops on "teaching writing" and "reading fluency" for middle and high school students. I thought to myself, "This is all great stuff, but if I can't get my students to trust me or each other, none of it will work." After reading more about culturally responsive teaching, I realized that one of our essential jobs as teachers is to bring out our students' authentic selves in the classroom.

As an English teacher, I wanted nothing more than to teach Shakespeare, the creation stories, Greek mythology, and existential poetry—the subjects that excited me so much in college. Unfortunately, these subjects were of little interest or relevance to most of my students, who were much more concerned with acclimating to a new environment. Some of my students were so disinterested with school that they actively sought detention, which they hoped would lead to suspension and, eventually, expulsion.

How, I wondered, could teachers best create dynamic learning environments that speak to *all* our students? How might we build relationships in the classroom with and among students of different ethnic, cultural, and life experiences? This book is my attempt to answer these vital questions.

Today's teachers are under extreme pressure to prove that they can grow children to new levels of knowledge, but teaching is a relational profession. There are elements of dignity and humanity to education that we can't forget about. We must do everything in our power to make connections—to show that we care—if our students are to succeed. I hope that this book will inspire and provide direction for teachers whose students may not look or sound like them.

Introduction

According to the Center for Public Education, U.S. classrooms consist more and more of black and Latino students (2007). By contrast, teacher demographics have remained overwhelmingly white (84 percent) and female (76 percent; the National Center for Education Statistics, 2016). These figures have hardly changed in the last 15 years. Educators must challenge themselves and their students to share personal and cultural information with one another, and must work to address learning gaps and resource inequities among different subgroups.

The Pursuit of Equity in Education

I once asked students in my 9th grade English class to reflect on and write about some memories from elementary school. Expecting them to write about academic or extracurricular achievements, I was taken aback to read the following response from one student:

> When I was in the 4th grade, my family was kicked out of the apartment we were living in after moving here from Mexico. I remember my mom leaving us. I remember needing to go live with abuela [grandma]. I remember my older brother would always stay out late. He'd then come home and beat me up for no reason. I was afraid of my brother. The 4th grade is when I started to sleep in the attic so my brother would no longer beat me up. I'd also hide up there from all my family drama. We were supposed to move to this country for a better life. . . .

This story reminds us that every single day children go to school struggling from family, economic, or social conditions that profoundly affect their ability to learn. Educators who focus solely on students' academic development without taking into account their lived reality outside of school are guilty of perpetuating a dehumanizing system with unwanted repercussions. The greatest threat to future generations—indeed, to the very foundations of democracy—is found in our too-often callous disregard for educational inequities. When schools don't treat students from different backgrounds fairly, neither does society at large.

Equity exists when teachers provide students with the tools they need to be successful not just academically, but also culturally and psychologically. If all students were alike, equity would simply be a matter of distributing resources equally to all students. Of course, every teacher knows that this is not the case. Individual students have vastly disparate needs that can radically affect the quality of their learning.

Culturally Responsive Teaching as a Means Toward Equity

To facilitate learning in multicultural classrooms, teachers must relate the content they teach to their students' cultural backgrounds. Before they can do this, however, they must first understand who their students really are. Geneva Gay (2000) teaches us that culturally responsive teaching connects students' cultural knowledge, prior experiences, and performance styles to academic knowledge and intellectual tools in ways that legitimize what students already know. And to address students' sociocultural realities through curriculum content, culturally responsive teachers must transcend their own inherent biases first.

Culturally responsive classrooms require careful planning and explicit teaching around social interactions so that students learn to assume responsibility for their learning, feel comfortable exploring differences of opinion, and accept that they may need help from their classmates to be successful. Teachers in these classrooms help to bridge different ways of knowing and engage students from nondominant cultures as they develop proficiency with unfamiliar skills. Along the way, students learn to see the world from different perspectives and identify the risks of assuming privilege or power (or lack of either) in others—vital skills for success in the world beyond school.

To properly understand human development, we must consider it in a much broader context than that which can be immediately observed (Bronfenbrenner, 1977). Very often, the experiences our students have had at home or in their communities will indirectly manifest themselves in the classroom. Consider the following real-life example. One morning, I was visiting a 2nd grade classroom as children began to file in for the day. The teacher was counting heads, saying hello, and moving about the room. As she approached the coatroom, she noticed a group of girls giggling and squirming. Brandon, a skinny little boy in the class, had caught their attention by lifting his shirt to expose his belly. When the teacher noticed what Brandon was doing, she immediately reprimanded him.

"Excuse me! What do you think you're doing?" she yelled.

At that moment, every little head in the room turned to look at Brandon, who, without missing a beat, lifted his shirt and announced, "Check out my tight abs! No bullet could ever make its way through me!" The girls by the coatroom giggled again before scattering back to their seats.

Where does a 2nd grader learn to show off his body and discuss surviving a gunshot? Clearly, what Brandon has learned at home or in the community has made its way into the classroom space.

As classroom teachers, we can do our part, one classroom at a time, to ensure our students have equitable learning experiences. We can do our part to build authentic relationships with our students. The strategies presented in this text are meant to support teachers as they look for ideas to engage all students in real and relevant ways.

Now, reflect on the following questions:

- Where specifically would you assume that Brandon learned the behavior he exhibited in class?
- Why did Brandon's behavior make its way into the classroom?
- How might the teacher equitably intervene in this situation?
- What are some examples of students' outside lives manifesting themselves in your classroom or school?

CHAPTER 1

Self-Awareness: Relationship-Building in Diverse Classrooms

Every teacher understands that building positive relationships with students is essential to ensuring their success in school. Unfortunately, too many student-teacher relationships today are based on false pretenses or faulty assumptions; what a disservice we do to our students' potential when our perceptions of them are based only on rumor or asides from other teachers ("Oh, you've got *him* this year. Good luck!"). Creating successful and equitable learning environments for our students means committing to the fact that every learner has a compelling life story worth getting to know. Our role as teachers is to help students uncover, for themselves, how personal identities and learning habits developed outside of school might inform their success in the classroom.

Student Assumptions About Teachers: The Case of Ms. H

Just as teachers make assumptions about students, students, too, make assumptions about teachers. Building relationships in the classroom is a two-way street.

Consider the following example. A few years ago, during my time as a school administrator, a young teacher approached me in the hallway.

"Dr. Lopez," she said, "you wouldn't believe what just happened in my class! One of my students thought I was *rich!* We were discussing *The Great Gatsby*, and Miguel mentioned how white people have a lot of money—'Just like you, right Ms. H?,' he said. I told him the truth—that I live in my parents' basement and don't have any hot water!"

Ms. H was a white woman teaching in a predominately Latino school. Clearly, some students in her class associated her identity with wealth. I applauded Ms. H for her effort to continue the conversation with her students and to break down stereotypes. Though she wasn't entirely comfortable, Ms. H engaged her class in a dialogue about the dangers of making assumptions. At the same time, it occurred to me that it was April—why were her students only now discovering that she lived with her parents and had no hot water? To create an honest learning space, we need to begin unpacking assumptions and realities with students in our classrooms sooner rather than later.

What assumptions do you think students make of you? How have you engaged students in honest conversations regarding their assumptions about you versus the reality?

Self-Awareness Strategies: Unpacking Assumptions, Discovering Realties

Self-awareness is the ability to accurately judge one's own performance and behavior and to respond appropriately to different social situations—a skill vital to student success. The following activities for instilling self-awareness can help both students and teachers distinguish assumptions from realities in the classroom, and can lay the foundation for courageous conversations about race, socioeconomic status, and other such sensitive issues as the year goes on. I encourage teachers to conduct these activities alongside their students and to be the first to share their work.

Assumptions About My Teacher

Prior to meeting with your students, make a list of 8 to 10 questions about yourself that they will answer as a whole group. You may create a slideshow out of your questions or simply write them on the board. Some sample questions:

- Where do you think I was born?
- What's my favorite color?

- What's my favorite cartoon?
- What do you think I like to do for fun?
- What kind of car do you think I drive?

Have students respond to your questions and list all their responses on the board. After all the questions are answered, reveal the true answers to each of them one by one. Ask your students to reflect on their assumptions versus the realities. If students' assumptions were correct, ask them why they felt this was so.

Two Masks

Students create two different masks: one showing how others perceive them, and one showing how they feel on the inside. As the teacher, you should begin by sharing your masks with the whole group. (I have seen teachers draw witch-like features on the mask, showing how they're perceived, and music notes, pets, or children on the other mask.) Discuss with students how we often get so hung up on how we want others to "see us" that we fail to share our real selves. Students then break into pairs to discuss why they drew their masks the way they did. As you walk around, pay special attention to students who exhibit courage by sharing deep and perhaps uncomfortable feelings.

The Johari Window

Developed by U.S. psychologists Joseph Luft and Harry Ingham in the 1950s, the Johari Window is a simple strategy that teachers can use for understanding self-awareness and personal development, improving classroom communication, building interpersonal relationships, and fostering positive group dynamics. The idea is to have students fill in the four quadrants in Figure 1.1 and discuss in a small group or one-on-one with the teacher:

1. *The Public Self.* What is widely known both to us and to others (e.g., name, height, race, neighborhood).
2. *The Blind Self.* What others know about us, but that we don't know about ourselves (e.g., when a teacher sees in a student his ability to

FIGURE 1.1

The Johari Window

	What Others See in Me	What Others Do Not See in Me
What I See in Me	*The Public Self:*	*The Private Self:*
What I Do Not See in Me	*The Blind Self:*	*The Undiscovered Self:*

be a great leader or communicator, although the student does not see it in himself).

3. *The Private Self.* What we keep hidden from others (e.g., unpleasant feelings, insecurities, not-so-great experiences).
4. *The Undiscovered Self.* What neither we nor others know or recognize (e.g., undiscovered skills or potential).

Distribute a handout of the Johari Window to all students and talk them through each of the four quadrants as they fill them in. In discussing each of the quadrants, both you and your students gain a better appreciation for what other people do and don't see in them. Though students may initially be wary about sharing, collaborative discussion usually leads to more and more opening up. As students provide one another with feedback, they start to see themselves through one another's eyes. Moving from one quadrant to the next together allows students to develop mutual trust, share hopes and dreams, and find things in common.

The process of collaborating on the Johari Window activity mirrors what happens more broadly over time in school: students and teachers become more comfortable with one another and with revealing more and more about themselves.

Rules of Engagement

This activity is meant to prime students for engaging in safe and respect-ful classroom conversations. It's a good idea to do this activity at the begin-ning of the school year or in response to incidents of bullying or intolerance.

Begin by having students break into small groups. Then share the fol-lowing prompt, either on a handout or on the board: *What will it take for you to feel safe and comfortable when having conversations about race, ethnicity, or culture?* In their groups, students discuss and create lists of 5 to 10 rules for feeling safe and comfortable in such situations. When they're done, choose five volunteers to share their rules. You can then create a large poster featuring the shared rules.

Here are some examples of rules of engagement that I've seen students come up with:

- Listen with an open mind.
- Don't call people names.
- Be open to constructive criticism.
- Make sure conversations are open to everyone.
- Don't use bad words.
- Respect those who are speaking.
- Be willing to see multiple points of view.

Minority-Majority Moments

This strategy is suitable for older students, as well as for teachers and school leaders. Before conducting the activity, ensure that the group has completed the Rules of Engagement activity, which will help them set the tone and create a safe space for conversations.

The Minority-Majority Moments activity allows individuals to discuss times when they've felt like part of a minority or a majority. These discussions help participants develop understanding of and empathy for one another and have a long-lasting effect throughout the school year. To begin, participants spend 5 to 10 minutes reflecting on and writing about one time they were in a minority and one time they were in a majority. Then, either in small groups or as a whole group, students discuss the experiences they wrote about.

Student Assumptions About Teachers: The Case of Mr. B

Mr. B was a white man teaching in a predominantly Latino high school. Every day, Mr. B would walk into his sixth-period class and hear his students telling jokes about his clothes, or his hair, or the brown paper bag he used to carry his lunch. The students were not so kind to Mr. B, but he kept showing up every day, trying really hard to engage his students with music, comics, fun articles—anything he could think of to "hook" his students.

One year, around the fourth week of school, Mr. B approached me. "Dr. Lopez, I've had it!" he said. "I don't know what to do. My students don't like me . . . and I'm really getting the feeling they don't trust me." He asked if I would sit in his classroom and observe him and his students. I agreed.

The next day, I sat in on Mr. B's sixth-period class. Mr. B was at the front of the room writing the day's objectives on the board and greeting the students as they walked in. I noticed that when he'd turn his back to write, a couple of students standing behind him would hike their pants up in a "nerd-like" fashion and point their fingers at the rest of the students, who would laugh. Throughout the class period, students would make fun of the way Mr. B talked, speaking in exaggeratedly nasal voices. At one point, when students were working in small groups, someone threw some balled-up paper across the room, hitting Mr. B in the head. Mr. B gave me a look—*Do you see what I mean?*—and yelled at his students to cut it out. Two students responded by repeating Mr. B in a mocking tone.

Mr. B needed help with classroom management, that was for sure. But something else was going on: it seemed as though some students really wanted to engage, but were just too distracted.

After class, I sat with Mr. B and asked him where he thought he was losing his students. He mentioned his grouping technique, discussed the flow of his instruction, and then commented on the two boys in front of the class who were making fun of him. I asked him to elaborate on that. He thought for a moment before answering: "They keep mocking me like I'm some white guy." Mr. B was frustrated that his students didn't know who he really was. I challenged him to start class the next day with a conversation about who he and his students really are.

What happened next and over the course of the school year astounded me.

As I sat in the back of Mr. B's room the next day, students filed into the classroom and were greeted by the following question on the board: "Am I a white man?"

Some of the students looked perplexed. When the two troublemakers from the day before entered, they read the question and quickly answered out loud: "Hell yeah, you're a white man!"

Mr. B told the boys to sit down. "What makes me a white man?" he asked.

The students started murmuring among themselves. One said, "You're white, and you sound like white people."

Patiently and calmly, Mr. B pushed for more information. "What does it mean to sound white?" he asked.

The conversation opened up as more students joined in. A debate soon formed about sounding "white" versus "Mexican" or "Puerto Rican." The conversation then turned back to Mr. B, unveiling assumptions about where Mr. B was born, the types of music he liked, and more. The more Mr. B revealed about himself, the more they, too, opened up about their home environments and personal experiences they'd had related to their ethnicity. Mr. B needed to enter a courageous conversation with his students to unpack some of his own assumptions as well. Eventually, the conversation turned to the importance of engaging in safe but uncomfortable dialogue.

Do you know what you "sound like" to your students? In what ways have you engaged your students in conversations about race and identity in your classroom?

7

Helping Students Develop Their Cultural Identities

It is important for us as educators to help students feel comfortable with their cultural identities. Students should feel comfortable sharing and describing their cultural traditions in the classroom. Everyone's identities adapt and change throughout their lives in response to political, economic, educational, and social experiences (Gollnick & Chinn, 2002). Students' self-awareness of their cultural identities provides them with a foundation for defining their true selves. Teachers should openly embrace cultural diversity in their classrooms and help validate students' constructed identities. Doing this can lead students to appreciate and celebrate their differences.

Pursuing self-awareness and identity work in the classroom can sometimes feel daunting or difficult, especially as the pressure to increase rigor and meet mandated standards builds.

Summary

Educators know that we must build safe classroom learning spaces and that we must be deliberate about teaching and engaging in self-awareness strategies with students. The strategies presented in this chapter can help teachers develop a far greater understanding and respect for who their students really are, peeling away at real or perceived inequities before they take root. Bear in mind that these strategies are more than mere icebreaker activities—they should occur often throughout the school year. Regular and deep conversations about culture, race, and identity are also necessary for authentic and equitable learning to flourish in the classroom. Students with strong self-awareness skills should be able to:

- Recognize the needs of peers who may be struggling in some academic areas;
- Respect the cultural and religious values of others in the classroom;
- Reflect on and express how their behaviors and words can affect others;

- Display an ability to understand and articulate their feelings;
- Use self-instruction (e.g., "First we'll do this, then we'll do that") to solve social or academic problems;
- Identify what they must learn in order to complete individual or group tasks successfully;
- Understand their personal strengths and weaknesses and feel comfortable articulating them with others; and
- Express their cultural identities with pride.

In Chapter 2, I discuss how teachers can further enhance classroom relationships and collaborations with and among their students while maintaining a focus on equity and cultural responsiveness. I will share strategies teachers can use to design a successful learning environment and to leverage the classroom space so that students can experience valuable epiphanies about their learning styles and behaviors.

CHAPTER 2

Designing and Leveraging an Effective Learning Environment

In this chapter, we continue our discussion of self-awareness, individuality, and social-emotional learning, but more specifically address how teachers can find time in their schedules to enhance and leverage the classroom environment to help them and their students get to the root of classroom behaviors.

There is a great deal of research about the effects of the immediate environment on student learning. Strange and Banning (2001) note that physical spaces can be as welcoming or discouraging, valuing or disrespecting, as verbal messages. Strange and Banning (2001, 2015) cite research that links the physical attractiveness and lighting of a space to the motivation and task performance of those in it. Scott-Webber, Strickland, and Kapitula (2013) note that physical spaces have a distinct effect on knowledge creation, communication, and application, exerting a powerful influence on learning activities.

In my early days an educator, I was hired to teach 10th grade English at a newly opened urban high school. I came on board as the school was inaugurating its first sophomore class. My first impressions of the building were great: it was only two years old and immaculate—long, bright hallways and clean, open spaces. The school stood proudly as a beacon of hope in the middle of a community long ravaged by gangs, drugs, and violence. From the outside, and to the untrained eye, the building was perfect. There was only one problem: no one ever asked the children, parents, or community for input on what *they* wanted to see in the school.

As I began my work in the fall, small things began to catch my attention. I noticed that the school's lockers were very small. I remember one student saying, "Look, Mr. Lopez, I can't even fit my gym shoe in!" It was funny to the student, but not so much to us teachers. In the classrooms, there was barely any storage space for students or teachers—and classrooms themselves were scarce to begin with. The hallways were so narrow that going from one point to another inevitably resulted in shoving matches. Educators at this school had to work very hard to make do with what we had. Ultimately, the layout of the school impacted student learning in that we had more students arriving late to class, shoving matches in the hall resulted in more students being out of the classroom, and the cinder-block walls had the effect of making students feel caged in.

Still, regardless of dimensions, we as educators do have the power to control and design the spaces we are given—and when we include students in the design process, we grant them a degree of ownership over their learning environment. If we truly believe that all children should have a voice in their learning, we must also grant them a voice in managing the physical space in which learning happens. When students see their interests, backgrounds, and cultures reflected on the walls of the classroom, they are bound to feel more welcome and comfortable engaging with schoolwork. Such an environment contributes greatly both to academic and emotional growth.

In my experience, there are three must-haves for enhancing the learning space to maximize learning:

1. Input from students;
2. Attention to students' well-being; and
3. Enthusiasm for students' ideas.

Input from Students

A few years ago, I was working with an elementary school in Chicago, helping the teachers think through ways they might best leverage their physical spaces for student success. On one of my rounds, I walked into a

4th grade classroom, where students were studying U.S. geography. During class discussion, one student mentioned wanting to "see" the United States. A recent immigrant, the student was having trouble picturing where the country was in relation to others. He had an idea. "What if we got a large area rug that showed us the different states?" he asked. "That way we could stand in Illinois and walk to Florida."

The teacher looked straight at me.

"Good question, Javier," she said. Then she turned to me again.

"Dr. Lopez, what do you think about finding us a large area rug with the states on it?" She turned back to the class. "Dr. Lopez is big on adding things to the classroom 'space,' so maybe he can help us."

The teacher's sarcasm was inescapable and stemmed from an earlier meeting in which we'd disagreed about allowing students control of designing the learning space. She argued that only teachers should have a say in the matter.

"That's a great idea," I answered. "I'll see what I can find."

I should probably have thought a bit more before speaking, as I had no idea where the funds for such a rug would come from. Nevertheless, we were eventually able to find a large rug featuring a map of the United States for the class. The message this sent to students was simple but profound: "We, the educators, believe that you, the students, can and should help design learning spaces for yourself and for everyone around you."

Attention to Students' Well-Being

A week or so later, word had gotten out that I'd helped secure a rug for the 4th grade class. One morning, a 2nd grade teacher approached me.

"I heard you got the 4th grade class a rug for their classroom! You know, I've been asking the administration to move the piano in room 105 to my room." The old piano had been gathering dust, untuned and unplayed, for years. "I play the piano and would love to incorporate some music in my class." She batted her eyes and smiled. "Maybe you can get it for me?"

I should have known then not to honor the teacher's request, but I was thinking how cool it would be for students to interact with live music in a 2nd grade classroom. However, unlike the previous request for the rug, this one was initiated by a teacher rather than the students. I should have taken this red flag into account.

A week later, I received permission to move the piano into the 2nd grade classroom. Two weeks after that, I asked around to see if teachers with classrooms nearby ever heard music playing. Most of them said no. One day, I walked into the 2nd grade classroom and noticed that the piano was tucked nicely into a corner. Protruding from behind the piano were two little feet. I asked the teacher to explain.

"Oh, that's Isaiah!" she said. "Isaiah needs to learn some manners, so he is taking a time out behind the piano."

I almost fainted when I heard this.

"Behind the piano?!" I said, incredulously. Some of the students smirked at me. All I could think about was how poor Isaiah was going to grow up to hate pianos!

Enthusiasm for Students' Ideas

I've been in many classrooms where a student will have his or her hand raised for quite some time and never be called upon. At the end of the class, I'll ask the teacher why the student was ignored. The response is often along the same lines: "If I call on that kid, he or she will say something silly and throw the whole lesson off track."

It's true that silliness can upend our lessons, but it's important for us to understand the difference between kidding around to be disruptive and doing so out of genuine curiosity about things. Once, in a kindergarten classroom, I observed as the teacher read aloud to her students, who were seated in a circle on the floor, from the book *Pinkalicious* by Victoria and Elizabeth Kann. When the teacher was done reading, a child raised her hand eagerly. The teacher called on her, and she stood up with a dreamy look in her eyes.

"Ms. C.," she said, "what if we could paint one of the classroom walls pink? Wouldn't that be great? Then we could decorate it with cupcakes, just like in the book!"

"I'm not sure that's a good idea," replied the teacher. "Do you know how much money it would cost to paint an entire wall pink?"

The poor kindergarten dreamer was crushed. Later, the teacher would tell me that she was trying to make a case for understanding how much things cost, but the truth of the matter was that the teacher did not show that she valued the student's vision. I explained to her that children's dreams and ideas are like bubbles of creativity in their minds, and that it's not our job to take a hammer to them; rather, we must respect students' visions and offer suggestions for helping to meet them.

"Well, I guess I could have alluded to something else that's pink in the classroom," responded the teacher. "Or I could have suggested that instead of painting the walls pink, we could hang some pink sashes around the room."

Five Principles for Creating a Comfortable Space for Diverse Students

By adhering to the following five principles, teachers can ensure that their classrooms work toward, rather than against, student learning.

1. Flexibility

Students should be able to shift from listening to a teacher lecture to working in groups to working independently with ease. To this end, it makes sense to construct spaces that can be quickly reconfigured to support different kinds of activities (e.g., moveable tables and chairs, whiteboards on various walls, classroom partitions).

2. Comfort

I remember teaching a 10th grade English class and noticing that one of my students seemed totally disinterested in a group activity we were working on. I asked him what was wrong.

"It's not you or the lesson," he said. "I just feel so uncomfortable in these hard chairs!"

I couldn't blame him—the chairs in the room really weren't comfortable at all. As a group, the students decided to move over by a large window area, where they could all stand or sit on padded seats. Comfort is extremely important for learning.

3. Sensory Stimulation

We all know we need to keep our classrooms clean, but we must take care not to go too far and create a completely antiseptic environment. Our students yearn for color, natural and task-appropriate lighting, and interesting shapes to keep them stimulated. Students today are accustomed to seeing creative uses of space on TV remodeling shows and in big-box stores (to name just two examples). And some, particularly those living in poverty or with difficult home lives, are all too accustomed to rearranging their environments. Be sure to take into account students' identities and cultures when decorating a stimulating learning space.

4. Technology Support

If you haven't noticed already, the current generation of students expects seamless technology integration in the classroom, including Wi-Fi and access to charging stations. Rather than rely on cumbersome rack systems and fixed ceiling-mounted projectors, contemporary learning spaces must include plug-and-play capabilities.

5. De-Centeredness

Within the classroom, teachers must avoid sending the message that the teacher's space is somehow privileged (e.g., at the front of the class). Outside the classroom, de-centeredness means providing a variety of locales around the school for discussion, engagement, and study. Corridors and outdoor passageways should be designed to encourage ease of movement from one learning space to another.

Reflection Questions

1. How does the layout of your classroom affect students' learning?

2. What items are on the walls of your classroom? Are these items store-bought? Student-made?

3. Do students see their own cultures on the walls?

4. Describe a time when a student in your classroom wanted to add something to the learning space. Were you able to make it happen?

5. Do you think your students feel welcome in your classroom? How do you know?

6. Think back to Isaiah behind the piano. What other types of harm—short-term or long-term, mental, emotional, or physical—might we unwittingly inflict on our students in leveraging the classroom space?

7. How do students contribute to the design of your classroom?

8. If moving the desks or chairs around or writing on the walls are not options, what are other ways students can have a say in the design of their learning spaces?

9. How should the increasing diversity of our student populations affect how we think about the classroom environment?

10. How do you acknowledge students' cultures and identities in the physical learning space?

CHAPTER 3

Reality Therapy in Diverse Classrooms

We often tell our students over and over to correct their behavior—"Stop running in the halls!" "Lower your voices!"—with little or no result. The key to success here is to help your students walk into learning epiphanies—those "aha" revelations—about their behavior. In this chapter, we'll explore the difference between telling and showing students how to acknowledge and correct their behaviors in culturally responsive ways.

Whenever I discuss the topic of walking students into learning epiphanies, I like to tell a story from my childhood. Though I wasn't a terrible child, I certainly wasn't the best at following all the rules that my mom and dad had laid out for me. My father was on his feet all day at work and liked nothing more than to relax in silence when he'd get home. Unfortunately, when my sister and I were around eight or nine, we had a habit of running around the house playing tag. Inevitably, the simple act of tagging one another would escalate into full-scale hitting and a fight would break out between us.

Though my parents never hit us, they were very good at communicating their boundaries. I'll never forget the day a game of tag with my sister became particularly disruptive and my father exploded.

"That's it!" he yelled. "I've had it!"

Then he took off his belt, at which point my sister and I started freaking out. He walked us both to the kitchen, rummaged for a nail, and hung his belt on the wall—a symbol, if you will, of peace and punishment, and a message that he and my mom were watching us. Though my father never hit us with the belt, you can be sure that the mere sight of it made us reflect and slow down whenever we'd rowdily pass by it.

There was something about the black belt hanging in the kitchen that altered the space, thereby affecting our behavior. As an educator, I've always strived to alter the classroom space as consequentially as my father altered the kitchen space. I certainly don't advocate hanging belts on the wall, but I do challenge teachers to consider how the items they affix around the room might affect student learning.

Reality Therapy

In the 1960s, psychologist William Glasser developed a counseling approach known as *reality therapy* (Glasser, 1965). What set this type of therapy apart from others is that it focused on three human principles—realism, responsibility, and right and wrong—rather than on symptoms of mental disorders. In education, reality therapy focuses on the immediate actions of students rather than on past events. It is a cognitive-behavioral approach to learning that helps students become more aware of their thoughts, actions, and surroundings (Henderson & Thomson, 2007). The example that follows shows how I have applied the approach with my students.

Walking into an Epiphany: The Case of Miguel

I had a 10th grade student a few years ago named Miguel. He was a tall, skinny, constantly disruptive loudmouth who didn't do much work. Among other things, he cussed so much that sometimes I thought he didn't even realize he was doing it.

At the beginning of the year, I did my best to get to learn more about who Miguel really was. I found out that he lived with his mom, who was quite young and dated a lot. Miguel and his mom didn't have a lot of money, but they did have a lot of family members who cared for them.

Because I had a rambunctious group of students who liked to bicker and fight with each other, one of my go-to teaching strategies was the Socratic method, whereby students follow a particular set of rules when engaging with one another on a particular text (e.g., formulating comments as, "What I think I hear you are saying is _____, but what I believe is _____").

One day, while studying *Macbeth,* Stephanie, a bright-eyed, curly-haired student sitting near the front of the room, was discussing the potential connection between diseases of Shakespeare's time and Macbeth's vision of Banquo's ghost in Act 3. She noted that fear of ghosts and death was rampant in Elizabethan times.

As Stephanie spoke, Miguel began shaking his head. When she was finished, I could barely keep him from jumping out of his seat.

"Mr. Lopez, I gotta come back to that," he said.

I reminded Miguel of the rules for Socratic discussion. He said "OK," and proceeded.

"What I think I hear Stephanie saying is that both Shakespeare and Macbeth are a bunch of little bitches!"

The class erupted in laughter, my jaw dropped, and Stephanie's face was red with anger. I reminded Miguel immediately of the classroom rules about swearing in class. After the bell rang, I let him know that I was going to call his mom that evening, and I did. When I had finished relaying to her what had happened, she had a very telling response.

"Why, that little motherfucker!" she cried.

At that moment I made the connection between Miguel's classroom behavior and his life at home. For Miguel, swearing was a completely normal aspect of his home space—which is why he genuinely seemed not to think he was doing anything wrong when he swore in class. My job was to walk Miguel into the epiphany of realizing that his behavior in the classroom was inappropriate. Scolding him over and over again wasn't going to do any good; my reprimands could never compete with the force of what was normal in his home life.

The next day, I set aside *Macbeth* for a discussion of classroom etiquette. I began by showing my students an image of the Motion Picture Association of America's (MPAA) rating system for movies (see Figure 3.1). Then I asked them to break into groups and discuss what would it mean to sound G-rated in class. After convening for a couple of minutes, the groups

FIGURE 3.1	
MPAA Ratings Adapted for the Classroom	
Rating	**Meaning**
G	General Audiences—for everyone to hear (including your little sister)
PG	Parental Guidance Suggested
PG-13	Parents Strongly Cautioned
R	Restricted—think very carefully before using!

shared their responses, which I wrote down. We then repeated the process for all the MPAA ratings. When everyone was done sharing, I hung the image of the rating system on the classroom wall and reminded the students that they were to "keep it PG" at all times. The students found this funny, but they went along with it.

A week or so later, the students were engaged in group projects and becoming increasingly loud and distracted. It was one of those days when the room seemed to slip away from me—as I worked one-on-one with individual students, the rest of the class began descending into chaos. When I realized that things were out of control, I became upset, but I was determined not to lose it. I stepped back behind my desk to regroup my thoughts and consider my options. I must have closed my eyes for a second, and I must have looked angry or frustrated, because at that very moment Miguel stood up at his desk to loudly address the entire class.

"You all need to be quiet before I go rated R up in here!" he yelled.

The students quieted down and turned to see what my reaction would be.

I walked over to Miguel and gave him a hug. After telling me to lay off him, he asked why I'd done that.

"Because you thought before you spoke," I said.

I was truly impressed that Miguel consciously thought not to curse. The use of the MPAA rating system had altered his space enough that he was able to walk into the epiphany of understanding that certain behaviors were unacceptable in the classroom.

Miguel's story is a good illustration of how important it is to create a space that encourages students to have their own epiphanies about learning and classroom behavior. It's worth noting that I wasn't able to fully grasp what was happening with Miguel until I took the time to build a relationship with him and learn not just about his mother, but also about his brothers, who had been in and out of jail. We're taught as teachers to pick our battles, and I could have just ignored his cussing, but I chose not to because his behavior was having an effect on others in the class. Girls, in particular, were a frequent target of Miguel's outbursts, which affected their concentration in class (not to mention demeaning them personally).

Miguel's triumph wasn't that he stopped swearing, but that he finally walked into the epiphany that he could pay attention to and alter his behavior to suit different environments.

Strategies for Altering the Classroom Space to Encourage Student Epiphanies

The following list of strategies for incorporating visuals in the classroom may be useful in helping your students walk into their own epiphanies. Bear in mind, however, that it is only after we have accurately assessed our students' backgrounds and learning needs that we can tailor these strategies for optimal effect.

Pick Up Your Pants

I have always found the trend among young men for wearing pants that sag far below the waistline distracting and disrespectful—and this was a battle that I chose to fight. I'd regularly say things to them like, "Where are your pants?" and "Do you *really* think that's stylish"? These types of interactions never ended well.

One day, I decided to alter the classroom space to help students walk into an epiphany about how to dress properly in the classroom. With the students' input, I created a poster showing how far below the point where I myself wore my pants constituted "decent" (see Figure 3.2). Thereafter, instead of scolding students, I'd ask them: "Hey, are you decent?" This one-word check worked wonders in my class. I no longer got into fights with my students, who learned to alter their dress for the classroom.

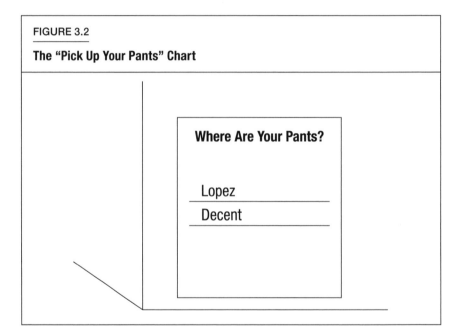

FIGURE 3.2

The "Pick Up Your Pants" Chart

Where Are Your Pants?

Lopez

Decent

The 90/10 Rule

I try to teach my students to understand that people are going to judge them based on their actions, and that their actions have consequences. Even some of my straight-A students have been sent to the office for misbehaving, often by teachers or other staff with preconceived ideas based on the way the students look. To help my students walk into the epiphany of thinking before escalating a situation, I have them reflect on and discuss the image in Figure 3.3, sharing examples of the 90/10 reaction/ performance ratio in their lives.

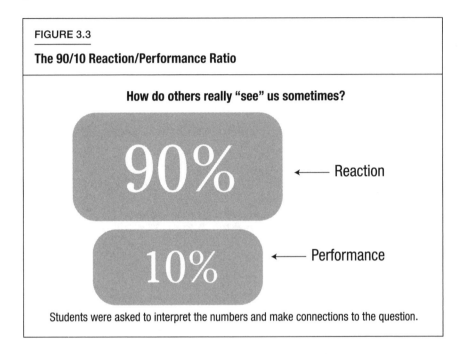

FIGURE 3.3

The 90/10 Reaction/Performance Ratio

How do others really "see" us sometimes?

90% ← Reaction

10% ← Performance

Students were asked to interpret the numbers and make connections to the question.

When we think about how others "see" us, 90 percent of the time people will judge you based on your actions or reactions to circumstances; they're sizing you up to see if they can trust you. Ten percent of the time, individuals will judge you based on what they think they know about your performance in a given area (Cuddy, 2012).

The Frog in the Well

Many students, particularly those living in poverty, are conditioned not to venture too far past their immediate street or neighborhood. To help spark their curiosity in the wider world, I like to tell them the story of the frog in the well:

There once was a frog who lived at the bottom of a well. This frog believed that he had everything in the world. One day, the frog noticed that there was an opening at the top of the well. *I wonder what lies beyond?* he thought to himself. Although he was scared, the frog decided to be brave and climb up to the opening.

When we reached the top, he couldn't believe what he saw. Outside of the well was a large pond surrounded by beautiful flowers and other living creatures. The frog realized that there was more to life than the well and decided to settle near the pond for some time. One day, after he'd become accustomed to his new surroundings, he noticed that there was a forest of trees on the horizon. He couldn't stop wondering what lay beyond the forest, so he once again decided to be brave and ventured off to find out.

After considerable exertion, the frog finally made it past the forest. To his amazement, he found himself in front of a large ocean. He had never seen so much water!

I typically stop telling the story here (much to my students' chagrin—they often want to know if the frog ends up surfing). At this point I ask my students to reflect on what the story is trying to teach us.

Summary

We, as teachers, need to be mindful of how best to leverage our classroom spaces for student success. It is our responsibility to help students walk into epiphanies related to their learning and behaviors—something we can only do well if we first forge meaningful relationships with them.

Reflection Questions

1. Can you think of a time when something was added to a space of yours (e.g., home, bedroom, classroom) that altered the way you behaved?

2. Have you added anything to your classroom recently that has altered your students' behavior?

3. Do your students know what they sound like or how they are behaving in your classroom environment?

4. Do you have any catchphrases, keywords, or gimmicks that you use in class to get students back on task?

5. Describe the difference between visual prompts intended to help students walk into epiphanies and charts that students alone create.

6. Do your students know what the purpose of the items on your class-room walls are?

7. What are the items on your walls really communicating to your students?

CHAPTER 4

Nonpunitive Interventions in Diverse Classrooms

In this chapter, we'll examine how building deep and meaningful relationships with students can facilitate nonpunitive interventions in the classroom. The ideas presented here are intended to help support a shift in mindset from punishing students to helping them walk into their epiphanies.

A note: I believe firmly that teachers should not do the work of developing culturally responsive nonpunitive interventions on their own. Consulting with other teachers, coaches, or mentors is critical if we are to succeed in our efforts.

The 10 Steps of Reality Therapy Counseling

Henderson and Thompson (2007) outline 10 steps and three phases for counseling students using reality therapy (see Chapter 3). Here, I adapt the steps and phases for use by classroom teachers.

Phase 1: Building a Better Relationship

Steps:

1. List what you have already tried but that didn't work for your student.
2. Make a list of change-of-pace interventions to disrupt the expected interactions between you and your student. For example, as it may be the case during your initial conversation with a student that the student is upset or uncomfortable, and in some instances may lash out in this early phase, it behooves us as teachers to "change the

pace" of the conversation and intervention. You might, perhaps, steer the conversation toward something personal, something that would help the student open up a bit more (say something such as, "I noticed you have a little brother"). While this thinking can then lead to step three, as teachers we should, when possible, think about potential "change-of-pace" interventions *prior* to engaging with the students. Toward that end, it would be helpful to know as much as possible about students' personal lives and realties at home.

3. Make a list of things you will do to help the student have a better day tomorrow. (If Phase 1 is unsuccessful, continue to the next phase.)

Phase 2: Counseling

Steps:

4. Ask the student to stop the undesirable behavior, providing him or her with desirable alternatives. Use as few words as possible, relying as much as you can on nonverbal gestures. Don't make any threats and acknowledge when the student cooperates.

5. Ask the student:
   - What did you do?
   - What were you supposed to do?
   - What could you do?
   - What will you do?

6. Through a handshake or written contract, affirm that the student will try to change the behavior. (If Phase 2 is unsuccessful, continue to the next phase.)

Phase 3: Addressing Chronically Disruptive Students

Steps:

7. For smaller children: Have the student sit in an assigned time-out chair or space inside the classroom. Have the student make a plan to return to the rest of the group while in time-out.

8. If a student needs to be excused from the classroom environment, he or she must understand why and must be able to develop a plan for rejoining the rest of the group.

9. Some children have difficulty going a whole day without disrupting the class. For these students, create individual educational plans (IEPs) listing four or five expectations that they are to meet every day. If the student does not meet one of these rules, have the parents or guardians remove the student from school for the day. (If the student's parents or guardians are not available, consider contacting a community agency.)

10. Take the student on a field trip to see the local juvenile court and observe the probable consequences of continued misbehavior. Try to set up meetings with judges, other court officials, and inmates.

The No-Punishment Empowerment Intervention (NPEI) Approach

Another way of helping students using the principles of reality therapy is the No-Punishment Empowerment Intervention (NPEI) approach, which has the following five steps:

1. Establish a relationship with the student. The more we, as teachers, know about our students' life experiences, the likelier we'll be to meet their classroom needs.

2. Focus on current behaviors rather than those of the past. This includes avoiding discussion of students' past behaviors with their previous teachers.

3. With the student's input, plan interventions that are likely to work.

4. Commit to carrying out the plan. This can be in the form of a verbal agreement, a handshake, or a written contract.

5. Do not punish the student if he or she doesn't abide by the plan. Instead, devise a new plan, again with the student's input. Insist that the student carry out the new plan or come up with a more feasible one.

The following true story of a 9th grade student who was chronically late to class illustrates the NPEI approach in action.

The Case of Stephanie

Stephanie, a Latina English-language learner with dark curly hair, was a good kid. Her only problem was that she was always late—every single day. Class started at 8 a.m., but she would inevitably run in around 8:15. The first time she showed up late, I assumed she'd been dilly-dallying in the hallway before class. In front of the other students, I told her that if she didn't start arriving on time, I would deduct participation points from her grade and give her detention. At the time I felt that I needed to set a tone, but in hindsight I was simply grandstanding—something I was guilty of doing many times early on in my career.

The second and third times Stephanie arrived to class late, I gave her detention and lowered her participation grade, just as I said I would. When I was driving home on the third day, I couldn't help thinking about Stephanie. Was there something I just wasn't getting? I had asked her several times to explain why she was late, but always in a stern voice that probably didn't sound very comforting to her ears.

The next day, as I was checking in at the main office, I ran into our social worker, Mr. A. I asked him if he knew anything about my student Stephanie. With 1,200 students in the school, I didn't really expect him to remember her, but Mr. A surprised me.

"Stephanie Aranda?" he said. "Sure, I know her and her family. Her mom goes to my church. They have a sad story: Stephanie has three older sisters and her mom's a drug addict. Stephanie's older sister is really trying her best to support her younger sisters and the family."

In the two minutes that I spent with Mr. A learning a little more about Stephanie's home life, I learned more about her than in the couple weeks I had had her in class.

Later that morning, when Stephanie once again rushed into class late, I made eye contact with her, but refrained from saying anything. Once the other students were busy with the day's work, I quietly approached Stephanie and asked if she would please see me after class for two minutes. Her face turned red, but she agreed.

After class, I began by asking Stephanie if she had older sisters. She looked at me funny, then responded that she had three. I asked her, "Are you late to class because of something going on at home? Are your sisters helping you?"

Her eyes opened wide. "Oh my gosh, Mr. Lopez!" she replied. "Yes! My sisters are always hogging the bathroom, so I'm always the last one to get in there, and then I gotta rush to catch the bus and get to school."

I nodded. "Is there something you can think of that you can do at home in the mornings so that you won't be late?" I asked.

At this point, many teachers would feel compelled to *tell* Stephanie what she should do to get to school on time—but it's much better to let her walk into her own epiphany. Stephanie thought for a bit before responding.

"I could probably get my clothes out and ready the night before," she said. "And I could get up a little earlier so that I can use the bathroom before my crazy sisters do."

My eyes lit up. I was impressed with Stephanie's ideas and wrote them down on a sticky note, along with the date and time. I signed the note and then asked Stephanie to do so as well.

"So what you're telling me," I said, "is that you want to get to school on time, but you always have to wait for your sisters to finish using the bathroom, causing you to be late. In order not be late, you're going to get your clothes ready the night before and get up a little earlier so you can be the first to use the bathroom. Correct?"

"Yes," replied Stephanie.

"Great," I said. I then apologized to Stephanie for not understanding her situation at home and for scolding her in front of the class. I wanted her to know that I was genuinely invested in her as a student and I really wanted nothing but the best for her.

The next morning at 8 a.m., I was standing in the hallway greeting my students as usual, but this time I eagerly kept an eye out for Stephanie. When the bell rang, I was disappointed—she was late once again.

At 8:09, the classroom door opened. It was Stephanie. She looked at me at the front of the room. As she was about to approach me, I shook my head and said, "I'm sorry, class has started. Please get to your seat."

Stephanie skulked to her seat in the back of the room. After class, as students were leaving, Stephanie came to my desk.

"I can't believe it, Stephanie," I said. "I thought we had this whole thing figured out. You said you were going to try something new—what happened?"

"Mr. Lopez, you're not even letting me talk," she said, then handed me a note. "Look at this note. I did everything we said. I'm trying—I really am. But this morning the stupid city bus was running late. I didn't think you'd believe me, so I asked the bus driver to write me a note backing me up."

She wasn't lying—that morning the city buses were indeed running late. Stephanie did do what she had said she would. I was so proud of her. I apologized for not listening and thanked her for really trying. She swelled with pride—not just for working to get to school on time, but also for getting at me for not listening.

Stephanie and I had very few problems the rest of the year. When she'd occasionally arrive late, we would revisit the intervention she had designed to see if any tweaks would help (e.g., going to bed earlier, asking others for a ride to school). It turned out to be a great year for Stephanie. Because she had a voice in finding a solution to her problem and because we had started to build a deep and meaningful relationship, she was more inclined to work on getting to school on time.

The NPEI Checklist

Use the checklist in Figure 4.1 and the NPEI Intervention Tool in Figure 4.2 to assist you as you use the NPEI approach with students.

FIGURE 4.1

NPEI Checklist

❐ I attempt to build strong relationships with my students.

❐ I attempt to fully understand my students' life experiences before punishing them for any infractions.

❐ My students contribute to the design of their own interventions.

❐ My students and I sign contracts affirming the interventions that we design together.

❐ Rather than punish my students when interventions fail, I review the interventions with them.

❐ If I have a conference with students, I call their parents.

❐ I have invited parents to meet with me and discuss their children's classroom issues.

FIGURE 4.2

NPEI Intervention Tool

This form can be modified to fit the needs of each student. The form can be filled out with the student, or teachers can have the student complete items 5, 6, 7, 8, and 9 and discuss the remainder of the form with the teacher.

	1. Name of student: Homeroom #:
	2. Name one personal thing I know about the student that he or she was willing to share with me (e.g., whether the student has a job):
	3. How do you know you've built a good relationship with the student?
Building Relationships	4. List any questions, concerns, or comments you have about your relationship with the student:

Student's Current Behavior	5. What is the reason for this intervention?
	6. How does the student behave before, during, and after class?
	7. What's the student's excuse for the infraction? (The student can fill in this section.)

(continued)

FIGURE 4.2

NPEI Intervention Tool *(continued)*

Planned Behavior	8. What is the student's preferred learning style (e.g., visual, written, lecture; ask the student to confirm)?
	9. Ask the student to suggest interventions for correcting the behavior. Together with the student, outline a plan for the intervention and describe it here:
Commitment to the Plan	10. The student commits to the planned intervention. **Student signature:**
	11. The teacher commits to the planned intervention. **Teacher signature:**

Revisit Plan/ New Plan	Revision #1	12. Has the student violated the plan? If so, how and to what degree?	
		13. Has the teacher revisited the original plan? (steps 1 thru 9)	
		14. To what degree has the student violated the previous plan? (Time, offense, etc.)	
		15. In addition to the first attempted intervention, what else has the student decided to do in order to intervene with the negative or inappropriate behavior? (Student can fill this section in.)	Student Initials: Teacher Initials: *Phone Call Home Needed*
	Revision #2	16. Has the student violated the original and revised plan? 17. Has the teacher revisited both plans? (steps 1 thru 9)	
		18. To what degree has the student violated the previous plan? (Time, offense, etc.)	
		19. In addition to the first and second attempted interventions, what else has the student decided to do in order to intervene with the negative or inappropriate behavior? (Student can fill this section in.)	Student Initials: Teacher Initials: *Phone Call Home Needed*

After the 3rd revisit of the intervention, teachers should follow all proper school protocols as listed in the Faculty Guidebook or Student Code of Conduct. Referral to the dean is warranted if at least three intervention plans have failed. This form should be copied, kept for the teacher's records, then submitted to the dean's office with a referral or tardy detention attached.

Summary

The best way to intervene with regard to students' behavior or academic performance is to learn about who our students really are. As teachers, we have to shed our biases to gain an understanding of our students, their cultures, the communities in which they live, and their living situations.

Reflection Questions

1. What questions do you ask your students when they're late to class?

2. How do students design their own interventions in your class?

3. How does building deep and meaningful relationships with students help in designing appropriate interventions?

CHAPTER 5

The Making of an Expert

How can we, as teachers, remain sensitive to the needs of our students and their families while at the same time provide them with the tools necessary to succeed in life? My approach has always been to believe that every single one of my students can and will become an expert in something one day. If we teach our students to exhibit the characteristics of experts at a young age, we can set them up for long-term success in the future. In this chapter, we will focus on the three strategies central to nurturing expertise:

1. Practicing with purpose;
2. Identifying mentors and key influencers; and
3. Understanding the importance of patience and time for gaining expertise.

Much of the material in this chapter is gleaned from the work of Ericsson, Prietula, and Cokely (2007) and from Covey's (1989, 2004) work on the seven habits of highly effective people. In this chapter, the strategies you can use with your students are interwoven into the vignettes and stories presented.

Practicing with Purpose

Believing that even the most chronically disruptive kids in our classrooms can succeed requires faith—and true faith requires that we both "walk the walk" and "talk the talk." True faith asks us not only to believe that our students can be successful, but to actively help them achieve success. If we just talk about wanting to be a better teacher, we'll never actually become one.

A couple of years ago, I was teaching a graduate course to several young, beginning teachers from a school in the middle of a turnaround effort. I attempted to walk the teachers into the epiphany that they have resources at hand for meeting challenges, in the form of other teachers at the school. (In my experience, novice teachers tend to automatically try reinventing the wheel whenever they encounter obstacles, rather than searching for existing assistance.)

"I always try asking for help from other teachers," said one teacher, "but I was informed that the physics teachers in my school are old and useless. They really don't help."

I asked the young teacher to think for a minute about what she had said. Had she actually sought help from the physics teachers? Had she even met them? Or had she simply believed what others had told her? Once she realized that the latter was the case, she rethought her situation.

Our work as teachers is often difficult, but it doesn't have to be *that* difficult. Very often, when things get tough for us, it's because we fail to put our *beliefs* into *action*. To become the best teachers possible, we must take action to discover for ourselves what we need to get better at—and to get better, we need to practice with purpose. Deliberate practice of this sort is absolutely necessary for gaining true expertise. As I once heard another teacher say, "Living in a cave does not make you a geologist." Practicing with purpose requires considerable specific and sustained efforts to improve where we need to.

Below are some strategies you can incorporate into your instructional repertoire for ensuring that students approach their practice with purpose.

Giving Students the "Right" Homework

When we give students homework, are we sure that it's relevant to their lives? I am reminded of the math homework my 5th grade daughter gets. She can complete a whole worksheet relatively quickly, but gets hung up on specific word problems. What's better: having students complete the whole worksheet every time, or concentrating on two or three specific skills that students need to develop?

Supplying Students with Quotes about Practicing with Purpose

One way to get students in the appropriate mindset for practicing with purpose is to supply them with quotes on the idea to reflect upon at the beginning of class. Here are some examples:

- "Not all practice makes you perfect. You need a particular kind of practice—deliberate practice—to develop expertise."
- "Deliberate practice entails considerable, specific, and sustained efforts to do something you can't do well—or even at all."
- "Research across domains shows that it is only by working at what you can't do that you turn into the expert you want to become."
- "Genuine experts don't just practice deliberately; they also think deliberately."

To make the quotes more relevant to students' interests, try using ones from writers, artists, athletes, performers, and so on who are popular with them. Remember, getting to know our students on a relational rather than a transactional level will help us get further faster with our students.

Identifying Mentors and Key Influencers

Many people have asked me, "Dr. Lopez, when did you become so interested in leadership and education?" The truth is, I've been blessed by the mentors and key influencers in my life. I come from a family of thinkers and preachers. My great-grandmother was a poet, my grandmother was a writer, my grandfather was a preacher, and my dad, although not licensed to preach, could lay down a good home-cooked sermon whenever my sister and I needed it.

Most importantly, I come from a family of "doers." I rarely paid attention to what people had to "tell" me when I was younger, but I was always tuned in to what they did—their actions. Here's an example. I remember going to a conference on teaching writing once and listening to a speaker. Although the information she imparted was valuable, what really stuck with me was the image of a woman standing calmly in front of a crowd, clear-minded, well-spoken, and passionate about her material. I told myself that one day I, too, wanted to stand in front of a crowd and lead strategy around advocacy, inspiration, family engagement, access to education, and equity.

Think back for a second to when you were younger—not at the words you heard, but at the actions and reactions of those around you. Can you picture your mom, dad, or someone else you know *doing something?* Can you picture your mom cooking in the kitchen, singing at church, laughing while playing a game with you? Can you remember your father fixing a leaky faucet or broken doorknob? Were your parents passionate about what they did? Now reflect: Is there passion in your current life? Do you bring positivity to others? Do you consider yourself a blessing for others every day?

I remember, when I was 16, watching my father work on his master's degree in our small Chicago apartment. I didn't pay attention much to the specifics of what he was doing, but I could see him reading and writing at the kitchen table and taping notes onto the kitchen wall. Later that June, I graduated from high school and my father received his master's. We still have pictures of the two of us in our caps and gowns. I know he must have told me a hundred times what he was studying, but as a teenager I paid no attention to his words. What I saw in him, however—his habits of mind, his focus, his perseverance, his passion—have stayed with me all my life and their example is responsible for much of the success I've enjoyed to this day.

To quote Ericsson, Prietula, and Cokely (2007), "If we analyze the development of well-known artists, we see that in almost every case the success of their entire career was dependent on the quality of their practicing. In practically every case, the practicing was constantly super-vised, either by a teacher or an assistant to the teacher"—that is to say, by a key influencer. Research shows that our success depends largely on the quality of the mentorship we receive at different stages in our lives. As children, our main academic mentors tend to be local teachers who can give generously of their time and praise. When we get older, we seek out more advanced teachers to continue improving. It is up to us to put our need for mentorship into action by making the effort to find new influencers in our lives.

Recall the old saying: "Tell me who you hang with, and I'll tell you who you are." I wonder how often we discuss friendship with our students. We tend to assume that they just naturally know how to make and keep friends, but this isn't true at all. It's hard to make friends, unless we deliberately take action by putting ourselves in situations where we might develop bonds with other people (e.g., by signing up for extracurricular activities). There is great power in peer influence, and it is our job as teachers to help students get to know one another—especially across different backgrounds and cultures.

The following strategies can help you create the conditions necessary for your students to walk into the epiphany that friends, families, and community can help us stay motivated to succeed in school and in life.

Activity: What We See Each Other Do

For this activity, have pairs of students role-play different scenarios between friends (e.g., a discussion between an angry friend and an apologetic friend). Students can also use this activity to deliberately practice their approaches to peers in fraught situations (e.g., by practicing how to say no when offered drugs). For smaller children, you might use puppets or characters glued on a stick to explore such scenarios as being called a name, feeling left out at recess, fighting over a toy, and so on.

Activity: Class Photo Book

This activity is suitable for any grade. It can be conducted at any point during the school year, although I recommend doing so right before or after a holiday break.

Begin by taking or collecting photos of each child in the class. Affix each photo to a blank page, then collate the pages to create a class photo book. Leave the book in a specific location so students can draw or write on one another's pages. Ask older students to write words on their classmates' pages that they associate with them. Students will enjoy seeing what their classmates are saying about them. At the end of the year, you can make a copy of the whole book for each student or give each student his or her page to take home.

Activity: The Keys to Friendship

This activity is particularly helpful when conflicts arise among friends in the class or when reading about such conflicts. On a poster board, write the heading, "The Keys to Being a Good Friend." Next, supply students with cardboard "keys" on which they are to write the characteristics they value most in their friends. The students then affix their "keys" to the poster board.

Activity: Developing Expertise

This activity will help get your students thinking about what it takes to become an expert in anything. The next time you study a celebrated individual in class, ask your students to consider *how* the person became accomplished. In groups of three or four, have students answer the following three questions:

1. Did the person approach his or her practice with purpose?
2. What friends, mentors, or teachers helped the person succeed in life?
3. Did the person rush to succeed, or take the time to do things right?

Alternatively, you can break the class into three groups, one for each of the three criteria for developing expertise. This can be a good priming activity before studying a specific character or figure. I have also seen teachers blend the activity into the class discussion. It is key to connect the learning back to the students by having them reflect on how the three principles work in their lives.

Understanding the Importance of Patience and Time for Gaining Expertise

We live in a time when young people want stuff and they want it fast. Entitlement encroaches on all facets of schooling and employment. Young people want to be recognized, promoted, and applauded for their "greatness" long before they've achieved it. It is imperative for us, as teachers, to help end this trend by walking our students into the epiphany that patience and time are essential for gaining expertise in any field of endeavor (Bryk, Gomez, Grunow, & LeMahieu, 2015; Collins, 2015; Vander Ark, 2012). Research shows that even the most gifted performers need a minimum of 10,000 hours of intense training before they are able to win big competitions (Ericsson, Ptrietula, & Cokely, 2007). If this is the case, then it makes sense to narrow the amount of yearly standards we expect our students to meet, so that they can take the time they need to truly absorb what they've learned.

Activity: Time Management Through Task Analysis

The following strategy can help you create the conditions necessary for your students to walk into the epiphany that patience and time are necessary factors for becoming experts on any given topic. Ask students to predict how long it will take to complete a task (e.g., riding a bike to a friend's house, making a sand castle, feeding the family pet). Then, have them complete the task and compare their estimated time with their predictions. Ask students to write down the various steps it took them to complete the task. The goal is to raise students' awareness of how important it is to accurately assess the amount of time needed to do something well. When students get the hang of this activity, transition to helping them manage their time on schoolwork.

Six Tips to Help Students Take Control of Their Time

Passing along to students the following tips will give them an appreciation of the importance of time management in the classroom:

1. **Make a to-do list each day.** Depending on the age and grade of your students, making a to-do list every day might be tricky—but it's not impossible. Learning to prioritize tasks is an essential skill. Some schools provide students with a calendar book for the year; I have seen teachers ask their students to write their tasks in those books to help them stay on track. Making a list of things to

be done on a given day can help increase student productivity. As well, students can be taught to reward themselves if they complete all the tasks on their list.

2. **Keep your work with you.** This is skill that students should master sooner rather than later. Students typically reach for their devices during a road trip or while in the waiting room at the doctor's office. Teaching students that it's OK to have their work with them at all times can help them learn a bit about time management—and perhaps they'll reach for their books rather than their devices if they find themselves with a little extra time.

3. **Don't be afraid to say "no."** Students will always have to deal with peer pressure. As young adults, we all wanted to hang out with our friends every chance we could. However, at some point, we came to understand the importance of priorities and became comfortable telling our friends "no"—and so should our students. Students must learn that it's OK to say "no" to friends asking them to go out and have ice cream when they know that they have a big test the next morning that they need to study for.

4. **Find your most productive time and place.** Some of us are most productive in the morning and some at night. The sooner students learn when they are most productive, the better. In line with teaching our students about when they are most productive is teaching them to determine *where* they are most comfortable studying. Students may be able to designate a place for study at home, at school, or at the library.

5. **Budget your time.** Students need not spend all of their time during the week studying. As many students are involved in weekly extracurricular activities—for example, sports, clubs—they may find it helpful to use a calendar to help them budget their time. In addition to scheduling time to study, urge students to schedule time for relaxation.

6. **Get a good night's sleep.** Sleep is important if your brain is to perform at its peak. Suggest to students that they list the things yet to be done on the next day's to-do list before they turn in for the night.

Summary

There are three essential criteria to becoming an expert:

1. Practicing with purpose;
2. Identifying mentors and key influencers; and
3. Understanding the importance of patience and time for gaining expertise.

These three actions can help both teachers and students think critically about their long-term success.

Reflection Questions

1. How does practicing with purpose relate to our work as teachers?

2. How does practicing with purpose relate to what we ask our students to do in the classroom?

3. Many students face situations in their personal lives that we could never dream of. How have you come to learn about the actions your students routinely see in their lives? How might this knowledge help us in our teaching?

4. How often do you have your students reflect on the mentors and key influencers in their lives?

5. How often do you ask your students to share the *actions* that they perceive both in and outside school?

6. How do you teach your students that even the most gifted and talented people in every field need to spend a lot of time in training and preparation?

CHAPTER 6

Work Ethic in Diverse Classrooms

According to Balfanz, Bridgeland, Bruce, and Fox (2013), high school graduation rates across the United States improved in the first decade of the
21st century. Researchers have noted that the number of "dropout factories"
(schools that fail to graduate more than 60 percent of students on time) in
the country dropped by more than 450 between 2002 and 2010 (Balfanz,
Bridgeland, Bruce, & Fox, 2013). Much of the credit for this goes to the
adoption of successful strategies for, among other things, helping students
read at grade level, implementing early warning systems to identify and
help struggling students, improving attendance, and creating alternative
learning opportunities. Most important of all, however, is helping students
develop a strong work ethic.

Students who lack a strong work ethic tend to demonstrate poor academic performance and often risk dropping out of school. Fortunately, over
the past few years, I have personally noticed an uptick in students from
traditionally low-performing schools making the leap toward success on
standardized assessments. But is this enough? An employer who hired several local high school students told me recently that these kids are "still
showing up late to work and with a poor attitude."

Two years ago, I had an opportunity to speak with district leaders
and school principals about post-secondary education initiatives. For the
most part, these educators were very proud of their students' scores on
state assessments. During my visit, I asked them to comment on how they
thought their graduates were performing in the "real world" today. Their

responses surprised me. Several of their students had been immediately employed in the local automotive industry, many went on to service jobs, and a handful enrolled in college. Leaders in the district made an effort to follow up with students' employers to see how they were faring. As it turned out, many of the employers they spoke with had concerns about their employees' work habits.

"I had a manager tell me that one kid was late almost every day," said one principal. "He was smart and he applied himself, but he couldn't manage to get to work on time." Another principal told the story of when a manager called him at the school, asking, "What are you doing to teach these kids how to cultivate a strong work ethic?"

My conversations with these school leaders have never left my mind. I recalled them when I heard from the mother of a student in Clinton Township, Michigan: "My son is just sleeping in the basement all day long," she said. "And this is a kid who got a 30 on the ACT. I thought everything at the school was going great. Because he was doing so well academically, I had no doubt he'd go to college and be a successful contributor to society. I was wrong. I think all the school cared about was getting him to pass those damned tests!"

Defining the Work Ethic

If educators want to get serious about instilling and promoting a work ethic in their schools, they must first clearly establish what they mean by the term, which dates at least to the early 1900s. In one small Wisconsin school district, I once asked a room full of K–8 teachers to define it. One teacher said it was "students' ability to commit to the tasks we give them." Another said, "It involves listening, being on time, and making connections to things outside of the classroom." As these responses show, teachers carry multiple beliefs about what it means to have a work ethic. Of course, as with every other skill discussed in this book, what we really want is for students to walk into their own epiphanies of what a work ethic represents.

The definition of a work ethic will vary by age and grade level, but there are some clear commonalities across the board. In 1930, Max Weber helped popularize the concept of the Protestant work ethic, which he partly defined as the extent to which a worker perceives his or her labor as satisfying and useful. This characteristic applies across ages and grade levels—after all, when we attach meaning to and derive satisfaction from learning, we value our work more—and is one of the four core strategies for helping students develop a strong work ethic:

1. Providing learning experiences that are satisfying, relevant, and useful;
2. Valuing consistency over speed;
3. Emphasizing honesty; and
4. Teaching the benefits of deferred gratification.

Work Ethic Strategy #1: Providing Learning Experiences That Are Satisfying, Relevant, and Useful

Not all schoolwork will automatically be "satisfying" to students, of course. This is why teachers try to incorporate diverse texts and strategies—to hook their students into enjoying the process of learning. Very often, students are conditioned to wait for the hook when a new lesson begins. Unfortunately, there are no "hooks" after graduation. This is why students need to learn to hook *themselves* on learning by homing in on what is most relevant and useful.

Balancing What's Satisfying and What's Useful

Recently, I observed a 5th grade class that was studying the human digestive system. It was the Tuesday after a long weekend, and the teacher had a great idea for satisfying her students' desire to discuss what they'd done, while also hooking them on the lesson. The first thing she had her students do that day was spend 10 minutes journaling about and discussing the role that their digestive systems played in their weekend. This question had students chuckling, but it also got them to think and write about concepts they had learned the week prior.

When the teacher asked the students to share with the whole class, one child, concerned about the junk food he'd eaten Sunday night, asked if it was possible to die of diarrhea. The other kids laughed, but the teacher took the opportunity to refresh the class on the science behind the digestive system to answer his question. (As it turns out, you *can* die of diarrhea.) In this case, the teacher was able, in the moment, to use an idea that piqued students' interest as a way of leading them to substantive learning.

Work Ethic Strategy #2: Valuing Consistency over Speed

Recently I read a book by Jim Collins (2012) titled *Great by Choice*. In the book, Collins speaks about leaders who, despite the collapse of the U.S. economy in recent years, not only remained successful in their leadership, but excelled to produce record-breaking profits. Collins's research points to one key motivating factor: consistency. He speaks about the "20-mile march": If two people walk across the country from San Francisco to the state of Maine, the person who keeps the most consistent daily pace—say, about 20 miles a day—will most likely arrive first. Why? Because of consistency and an understanding of the environment. A person who marches 40 miles in one day and then encounters unexpected bad weather may not have the energy to pull through, whereas the 20-mile marcher, who hasn't drained all his energy, can.

Most work that is completed hastily is of poor quality and not well-thought-out. If one of our goals as teachers is to walk our students into the epiphany that successful work involves preparation, focus, attention, and awareness of deadlines, then we must teach them that developing a consistent pace is much more effective than waiting until the last minute. As common and initially helpful as due dates for assignments can be, they represent a form of scaffolding that we want students to be able to do without over time as they develop a comfortable and effective working pace.

Work Ethic Strategy #3: Emphasizing Honesty

In our digital age, answers to questions can be found at the click of a mouse (or the touch of an iPad). The ability to plagiarize has become as simple as cutting and pasting. (I've even heard of students not bothering to change the typefaces and font sizes of the material they pilfer, making their dishonesty all that more obvious.) Now, more than ever, it is time for teachers to explicitly address the importance of truth-telling and the satisfaction that comes with honest effort.

Once, during a 9th grade lesson on Greek mythology, I saw a teacher ask students to read, one at a time, from a paper on Hades they'd been assigned to write. "Listen carefully," the teacher told the class. It soon became apparent that student after student was reading the exact same thing—they had all copied their material word for word from the same online description of Hades. The class began to sink. Then, one girl got up and said, "I don't know what you all are copying from, but here's what *I* got from the chapter." Her voice boomed in the room; the other students could sense her energy. When the girl was done reading from her non-plagiarized paper, the teacher turned to the rest of the class.

"Think about what Jasmine wrote," she said. "How did what she say make you feel? What is it about our own words that gets us moving?"

The class didn't respond. The teacher simply told the students to find the words in their papers that were theirs, and that if they couldn't find any, they needed to go back and add some. In this teachable moment, the teacher succeeded in walking her students into the epiphany that plagiarism was dishonest and, when rampant, could lead to indistinguishable work. As Jasmine showed, honest work is always more motivating and satisfying.

Work Ethic Strategy #4: Teaching the Benefits of Deferred Gratification

Completing tasks independently should feel good—but it can only be accomplished if we defer immediate gratification for the sake of the bigger picture. I have come across at least two different ways of explaining this notion of deferred gratification in the classroom. The first is probably the most common: by teaching students how to appreciate their own hard work. I've been in many classrooms where teachers have handed back assignments to students with no grades, only suggested revisions. The moans and groans from students of, "We have to do this again!" could be heard down the hall. Doing work over again is one thing; teaching students *what they can get out of it* is another. We need to let students know how great they're going to feel after applying themselves and doing their best work.

Another way to instill the value of deferred gratification in students is to contrast it with their sense of entitlement. Students will often complain when they don't receive As simply for showing up or doing what's asked of them. Why, they ask, can they not get the gratification of a good grade for doing the bare minimum? In these instances, we need to walk them into the epiphany that the *work* is what is meaningful, not the grade, and that we are most successful when we defer thought of the reward and focus our efforts on the task at hand.

As adults, we tend to find ways to sludge through work that we don't enjoy. Some of us set small rewards for ourselves for motivation. Two things I enjoy rewarding myself with are cold chocolate milk and some TV time. I tend to deprive myself of both if I'm working on a project, presentation, or grading papers. I purposely defer gratification until my work is complete. I've wondered lately: Who taught me that? Does everyone operate this way? Can this thinking help some students?

One powerful type of gratification that can greatly motivate students is a sense of pride in a job well done. It is, however, prudent to defer expressing such pride in some instances. For example, I once saw an 11th grader who did well on an assignment brag to his still-struggling peers, "I got this! You all can't even handle the way I write. You all are going to be stuck in summer school trying to figure this stuff out!" He laughed out loud. This student needed to be taught to defer the gratification of expressing his pride until his classmates had cause to join him.

Self-Monitoring Progress to Maintain a Strong Work Ethic

One important and effective way for students to develop a strong work ethic is to have them keep track of their own progress in the classroom. Some teachers require their students to keep journals in which they keep track of where they are in their work and how well they are doing.

I recall observing a 2nd grade classroom where the teacher asked her students to keep a progress-monitoring chart in the back of their notebooks. Students received monthly writing assignments with an emphasis on organization and grammar; the goal of the chart was for them to keep track of their own writing success. The teacher had developed a writing rubric on which students would receive varying scores for their writing assignments. (One student asked the teacher if he could visually depict his writing progress on the chart as an astronaut trying to reach the moon. The astronaut, he explained, would creep closer and closer to the moon as the student's writing progressed. The teacher agreed.)

Here's another example of self-monitoring in action and how it relates to work ethic. I once observed a 9th grade unit on *Lord of the Flies*. As students filed into the classroom, they noticed that the desks were pushed up against the walls. On the floor were a variety of supplies, including rolls of colored paper, markers, tape, glue, and scissors. As the students looked around, confused, Mr. B, who was sitting at his desk, simply told them to remain standing.

When the starting bell rang, Mr. B walked to the center of the room near the pile of materials. Reading from a piece of paper, he assigned students to groups of four or five. "This is your group," he said. "This is a pile of supplies. Your task is to make a working board game by the end of this class period." He provided no further instruction and returned to his desk.

The students looked at each other, dumbfounded. Some went up to Mr. B and asked for more information. His response was simple: "Make a game."

As the students worked, Mr. B sat at his desk taking notes. The students murmured to themselves: "What's he writing? Why's he taking notes? This is so weird." By the end of the period, most of the teams had succeeded in constructing a working board game using their limited resources. The students learned quickly that there was a connection between the scarcity of materials in the room and in the situation the characters find themselves in *Lord of the Flies*. As the students exited the classroom, Mr. B challenged them to think about what the game-making activity taught them about themselves.

The next day, many of the students were buzzing about the previous day's activity. The teacher handed out a notecard to all the students. On the card, he had listed the following words: *leader, bossy, follower, phone-talker, texter, thinker, doer, writer, speaker,* and *challenger.* He had the students circle the words that best described their behavior during the game-making activity.

"While you were working yesterday, I was taking notes," he said. "And I came up with these descriptions of you guys. Put the card away—we'll come back to it. I wanted to let you know that I wasn't grading you yesterday on your game. I was trying to assess your work ethic. Now I know, as we move through our work, the areas in which we all need support and growth."

The students got it. Some of the students shrank in their seats, a bit embarrassed, but Mr. B didn't call anyone out. He was deliberate in his instruction and the students, in that moment, could recognize themselves and others without saying much.

Ideas and Strategies for Assessing Student Work Ethic

Here are some ideas and strategies for assessing your students' work ethic development:

1. Explain to your students that you will expect a strong work ethic from them. Be sure they understand what your expectations are so they can self-monitor.
2. Teach students the four essential criteria of developing a strong work ethic: work that is satisfying and useful, valuing consistency over speed, exhibiting honesty, and deferring gratification. Create a self-assessment form for students to complete at the beginning of the year, middle of the year, and end of the year on which they can track their thinking about their work ethic development in these four areas.
3. Assess the following indicators of work ethic in students:
   – Punctuality
   – Regular assignment submission

- Being prepared for class
- Catching up on notes or assignments after an absence
- Participating in teamwork or group activities
- Maintaining a positive attitude toward learning

4. Angela Duckworth (2016) and others who write about work ethic, or grit, suggest having students self-assess on the following statements:
   - New ideas and projects sometimes distract me from previous ones.
   - Setbacks don't discourage me. I don't give up easily.
   - I often set a goal, but later choose to pursue a different one.
   - I am a hard worker.
   - I have difficulty maintaining my focus on projects that take more than a few months to complete.
   - I finish whatever I begin.
   - My interests change from year to year.
   - I am diligent. I never give up.
   - I have overcome setbacks to conquer an important challenge.

This assessment is usually provided in a Likert-scale format. Students can discuss in small groups or individually with their teacher.

Summary

We need to teach our kids to put in the backbone, the grit—the work ethic—to succeed in school and beyond. We don't have the luxury of hoping that they will intuitively learn positive work ethic habits; instead, we must deliberately teach them to value, self-monitor, and attempt to sustain a consistent and productive pace of work, not only for their academic success, but for their own personal enrichment as well.

Reflection Questions

1. What are some negative work habits that you have seen in your classroom? Are these apparent in other classrooms at your school? How do you know?

2. How do *you* define a positive work ethic? Would other teachers in your school agree with your definition?

3. What positive work habits do you deliberately teach in your classroom? How?

4. How would you describe the connection between work that is satisfying and work that is "useful" for your students?

5. How are you ensuring that student interest leads to substantive learning?

6. Describe what "consistency over speed" looks like in your classroom. Are students hurrying to turn their work in at the last minute, or are they budgeting their time more effectively?

7. What negative effects does rushing to complete work have on learning?

8. What interventions have you created to teach students the importance of consistency over speed in the classroom?

9. Describe how you teach honesty in your classroom.

10. What connections between honesty and work can students in your classroom make?

11. Are there cultural differences in students' understanding of "honesty"?

12. What are some definitions of *deferred gratification*?

13. What are some examples of deferred gratification that you have seen in your classroom?

14. Do different cultures defer gratification differently?

CHAPTER 7

Characteristics of Successful Teachers in Diverse Classrooms

When I was finishing my doctoral studies, I was asked to be part of a research study on the mentoring and induction of new teachers in Chicago's turnaround schools. I had the opportunity to work with several different teachers from three high schools and eight elementary schools that were going through reform. One year, almost half of the 30 teachers these schools had hired over the summer resigned their positions before the holiday break.

Of course, I wanted to know why all these teachers quit so soon. But after several failed attempts at contacting the teachers who resigned, I realized that it might be more important to understand why the teachers who *stayed* did so. That year, I learned to observe teachers in action and captured five characteristics that I have found are common to all teachers who are able to really reach kids, build relationships with them, and prove that they are actually learning:

1. They are self-aware.
2. In addition to being culturally responsive themselves, they teach students to be so as well.
3. They believe that all students can become experts one day.
4. They teach more than content and educate beyond the school walls.
5. They reflect on and find ways to prove their students' success.

Characteristic #1: Self-Awareness

In the first chapter of this book, we discussed the need for teachers to teach self-awareness or embed self-awareness strategies into their lessons and classrooms environments. Part of our work as teachers is to help students learn and get comfortable with their personal identities—their own cultures, languages, religions, and so on.

Having worked in several schools that have gone through upheaval at the faculty and administrative levels, I have observed time and again the constancy of our students' individuality. To walk students into related epiphanies, we, too, must exhibit a keen sense of own self-awareness. Do we really know what we sound like to our students? Do we really know what we look like to our students? Successful teachers know exactly how they come across in the classroom.

The Story of Miguel

Miguel, an 11th grader, was a good kid; he just needed, and asked for, a lot of attention. He was also often known for being late to class. One day, I observed as Miguel—pants sagging, a broad smile on his face—flung the door to class open nine minutes after the starting bell rang. He stood there at the threshold of the door with his hands on his hips, waiting for acknowledgment from his peers, who eventually started to chuckle.

At that moment, the teacher, Mrs. W, gave Miguel a sharp look and slammed the papers she was holding on her desk. She crossed her arms and stared at Miguel as he slowly made his way to his desk at the front of the room. He could see that Mrs. W was angry—and he was enjoying every second of it. She started walking toward him. He wasn't quite at his desk yet when he stopped and said, "Whoa, whoa! Mrs. W, you look angry!"

Mrs. W proceeded to remind Miguel about the classroom rules, though he was barely listening to her. Before he knew it, he was being kicked out of the class.

I like to tell this story because it shows how Mrs. W's approach actually fueled a bit of Miguel's behavior. The second Mrs. W slammed her papers down and crossed her arms, Miguel won. He wanted exactly that reaction from his teacher. When we talk about self-awareness, we're also talking about monitoring how we act in front of our students.

Characteristic #2: Teaching Students to Be Culturally Responsive

Successful teachers working in diverse learning environments are conscious of culturally responsive teaching (CRT) practices, but they also teach their students how to become more culturally responsive in their own lives. During one recent discussion of CRT with teachers in the Detroit area, several participants mentioned having their students complete various activities, such as placing items in a bag or box to represent their family heritage or cultures. Though I am in favor of such activities, I would ask teachers to complete a "decision tree" such as the one in Figure 7.1 before introducing them to the class.

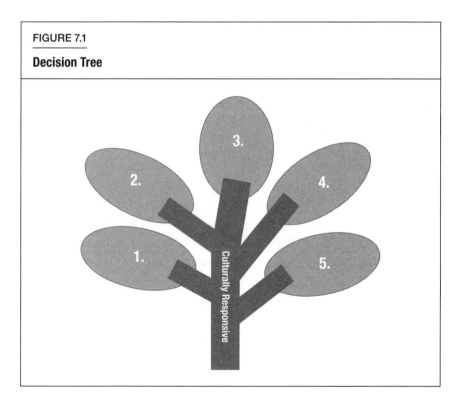

FIGURE 7.1

Decision Tree

The five steps I would include in my CRT decision tree are as follows:

1. Ask, "What are my thoughts, biases, and weakness when it comes to understanding the cultures that exist in my classroom?" and commit to address them.
2. Work with students to open up about (and demystify) their personal identities. (See the strategies in Chapter 1 for guidance with this process.)
3. Consider how to apply the new cultural knowledge to the learning space. Bring artifacts, ideas, and directions to the classroom that reflect students' identities.
4. Seek and highlight cultural connections to the curriculum.
5. Continually find ways to organically included CRT in your teaching throughout the year.

We want to create conditions in our classrooms where all students feel comfortable to question and learn about other individual cultures, customs, and languages without feeling as though it's taboo to bring anything up. Culturally responsive teaching happens when we, as teachers, continuously and deliberately bring it into the classroom.

Characteristic #3: Faith in Students' Potential

How we perceive our students' capacity to learn affects how we teach them. If we see them one-dimensionally, as thugs or even as criminals, then we start off believing they won't be able to succeed. Our role as teachers is to educate, and to educate we must believe that all our students can *and will* become experts in their chosen field one day.

Andre Perry, former Dean of Urban Education at Davenport University, once said, "The elimination of expulsion and suspension from discipline practices is the work that comes from a true faith that all children can learn" (Perry, 2016). It follows, then, that we must find ways to address behavioral issues in nonpunitive ways—and that when we don't know how to intervene, we ask colleagues for help.

Characteristic #4: Teaching More Than Content and Beyond the School Walls

A lot of the work I've done on my journey as an educator has been in the community surrounding these schools—often in community centers, the basements of local churches, or the homes of local leaders. The most powerful gatherings have always been those at which both community members and teachers were present. The teachers I know who have had the most success in challenging settings are those who have engaged deliberately in conversations with community organizations and faith-based leaders.

I recall watching Mrs. J, a 9th grade math teacher, give a great lesson one afternoon—then seeing her again after school at a meeting I had organized at the University of Chicago to discuss deeper practices for mentoring and supporting new teachers. I had mentioned the meeting to Mrs. J and, lo and behold, she came. This showed me just how engaged Mrs. J was with local events outside the school walls that could serve to help her teaching.

I understand that many of us have busy lives, but when an opportunity presents itself to speak knowledgably about school issues to the community and to public leaders, we should find the time to do so. In this regard, we teach more than content—we teach the truth about school realities to those with most at stake in it.

Characteristics #5: Reflecting On and Proving Student Success

By far, this is the characteristic I often talk about that turns the most heads. When I talk about *proving student success,* I don't necessarily mean testing. I believe in the value of assessments that help us make better decisions about instruction. However, I agree that in the last few years some school districts have taken these tools for teachers and turned them into compliance nightmares. We don't need 10 different assessment systems; we need the one right assessment system that will benefit our students.

Teachers who have been successful working in diverse classroom settings know how to interpret their data—and know what data isn't really important. They know not to get distracted by "noise" and focus on specific areas of academic development. When reflecting on data, bear in mind that the most successful teachers openly share what they've gleaned with colleagues to find solutions. The worst mistake we can make as teachers is to analyze data in isolation.

Conclusion

At the end of the day, our mission as teachers is to be of service to our students, their families, and the communities in which we teach. There are no golden tickets to ultimately being a successful teacher, but I hope the strategies, ideas, and lessons I've shared with you in this book support your work in helping *all* children succeed. Take the material in this book and share it, critique it, and use it in your classrooms, with faculty teams, during professional development, and so on.

Remember: don't go at this work alone. Teaching is a relational profession; as teachers we need one another—and all our students need us.

Bibliography

Balfanz, R., Bridgeland, J.M., Bruce, M., & Fox, J.H. (2013). Building a grad nation: Progress and challenge in ending the high school dropout epidemic. A report by Civic Enterprises Everyone Graduates Center at Johns Hopkins University America's Promise. Available: http://www. civicenterprises.net/MediaLibrary/Docs/17548_BGN_report_finalfull.pdf

Bandura, A. (2003). Social Cognitive Theory in cultural context. *Applied Psychology International Review, 51*(2), 269–291.

Barab, S.A., & Roth, W.M. (2006). Curriculum-based ecosystems: Supporting knowing from an ecological perspective. *Educational Researcher, 35*(5), 3–13.

Bransford, J.D., Brown, L.B., & Cocking, R.R. (2000). *How people learn: Brain, mind, experience, and school.* Washington, DC: National Academy Press.

Bronfenbrenner, U. (1977). Toward an experimental ecology of human development. *American Psychologist, 32*(7), 513–531.

Bronfenbrenner, U. (1986). Ecology of the family as a context for human development: Research perspectives. *Developmental Psychology, 22*(6), 723–742.

Bronfenbrenner, U. (1994). Ecological models of human development. In T. Husen & T.N. Postlethwaite (Eds.), *The international encyclopedia of education* (2nd ed., pp. 1643–1647). New York: Elsevier Science.

Bryk, A., Gomez, L.M., Grunow, A., & LeMahieu, P.G. (2015). *Learning to improve: How America's schools can get better at getting better.* Cambridge, MA: Harvard Education Press.

Collins, J., (2012). *Great by choice: Uncertainty, chaos, and luck: Why some thrive despite them all.* New York: Harper Collins Press.

Collins, J. (2015). *Good to great: Why some companies make the leap and others don't.* New York: Harper Business.

Covey, S. R. (2004). *The 7 habits of highly effective people.* New York: Simon & Schuster.

Crouch, R., & Zakariya, S. B. (2007). *The United States of education: The changing demographics of the United States and their schools.* Center for Public Education. Retrieved from http://www.centerforpubliceducation.org/You-May-Also-Be-Interested-In-landing-page-level/Organizing-a-School-YMABI/The-United-States-of-education-The-changing-demographics-of-the-United-States-and-their-schools.html

Cuddy, A. (2012). *First impressions: The science of meeting people.* Wired.com. Retrieved from https://www.wired.com/2012/11/amy-cuddy-first-impressions

Diller, D. (2008). *Spaces and places: Designing classrooms for literacy.* Portland, ME: Stenhouse.

Duckworth, A. (2016). *Grit: The power of passion and perseverance.* New York: Scribner.

Ericsson, K. A., Prietula, M. J., & Cokely, E. T. (2007). The making of an expert. *The Harvard Business Review, 85* (11), 1–8.

Gay, G. (2000). *Culturally responsive teaching, theory, research, and practice.* New York: Teacher College Press.

Glasser, W. (1965). *Reality therapy.* New York: Harper & Row.

Glasser, W. (1986). *Control theory in the classroom.* New York: Harper & Row.

Glasser, W. (1993). *The quality school teacher.* New York: HarperCollins.

Glasser, W. (1998). *Choice theory: A new psychology of personal freedom.* New York: HarperCollins.

Glasser, W. (2000). *Reality therapy in action.* New York: HarperCollins.

Glasser, W. (2002) *Unhappy teenagers: A way for parents and teachers to reach them.* New York: HarperCollins.

Gleason, S. C., & Gerzon, N. (2013). *Growing into equity: Professional learning and personalization in high-achieving schools.* Thousand Oaks, CA: Corwin.

Gollnick, D. M., & P. C. Chinn. (2002). *Multicultural education in a pluralistic society* (6th ed.). Upper Saddle River, NJ: Merrill.

Graetz, K. A., & Goliber, M. J. (2002). Designing collaborative learning places: Psychological foundations and new frontiers. In N. Van Note Chism and D. J. Bickford (Eds.), *The importance of physical space in creating supportive learning environments: New directions in teaching and learning, number 92* (pp. 13–22). Danvers, MA: Wiley Periodicals, Inc.

Hanson, P. (1973). The Johari Window: A model for soliciting and giving feedback. In J. Jones & J. W. Pfeiffer (Eds.), *The 1973 annual handbook for facilitators* (pp. 115–119). San Diego: Pfeiffer & Company.

Hattie, J. (2012). *Visible learning for teachers: Maximizing impact on learning.* London: Routledge.

Henderson, D. A. & Thompson, C. L. (2007). *Counseling children* (8th ed). Brooks/Cole. Boston: Cengage Learning.

Kuh, G. D., Kinzie, J., Schuh, J. H., Whitt, E. J., & Associates. (2005/2010). *Students' success in college: Creating the conditions that matter.* San Francisco: Jossey-Bass.

Lave, J., & Wenger, E. (1991). *Situated learning: Legitimate peripheral participation.* Cambridge, UK: Cambridge University Press.

Monahan, T. (2002). Flexible space & built pedagogy: Emerging IT embodiments. *Inventio, 4*(1), 1–19.

National Center for Education Statistics, U.S. Department of Education. (2016). Federal programs for education and related activities. In *Digest of education statistics.* Available: https://nces.ed.gov/programs/digest/d14/tables/dt14_209.10.asp?current=yes

Nucci, L. P. (2001). *Education in the moral domain.* Cambridge, UK: Cambridge University Press.

Oblinger, D. G. (2003). Boomers, gen-xers, and millennials: Understanding the "new students." *Educause Review, 38*(4), 37–47.

Oblinger, D. G. (2006). *Learning spaces.* Educause. Retrieved from http://net.educause.edu/ir/library/pdf/PUB7102.pdf

Omi, M. & Winant, H. (1994). *Racial formation in the United States: From the 1960s to the 1990s* (2nd ed., pp. 53–76). New York: Routledge.

Omi, M., & Winant, H. (2005). The theoretical status of the concept of race. In C. McCarthy, W. Crichlow, G. Dimitriadis, & N. Dolby (Eds.), *Race, identity, and representation in education* (2nd ed., pp. 3–12). London: Routledge.

Parker, W. (1996). Curriculum for democracy. In R. Soder (Ed.), *Democracy, education, and schooling* (pp. 182–210). San Francisco: Jossey-Bass.

Perry, A. (2016, May 17). *Do you really believe all children can learn? Then stop disciplining black students out of the system.* Retrieved from http://hechingerreport.org/really-believe-children-can-learn-stop-disciplining-black-students-system/

Scott-Webber, L., (2004). *In sync: Environment behavior research and the design of learning spaces.* Ann Arbor, MI: Society for College and University Planning.

Scott-Webber, L., Strickland, A., & Kapitula, R. (2013). Built environments impact behaviors: Results of an active learning post-occupancy evaluation. *Planning for Higher Education, 42*(1), 1–12.

Singleton, G. (2005). *Courageous conversations about race: A field guide for achieving equity in schools* (1st ed.). Thousand Oaks, CA: SAGE.

Singleton, G. E. (2013). *More conversations about race.* Thousand Oaks, CA: SAGE.

Strange, C. C., & Banning, J. H. (2001). *Educating by design: Creating campus learning environments that work.* San Francisco: Jossey-Bass.

Strange, C. C., & Banning, J. H. (2001/2015). *Designing for learning: Creating campus environments for student success.* San Francisco: Jossey-Bass.

Tomlinson, C. A. (2004). *How to differentiate instruction in mixed-ability classrooms.* Alexandria, VA: ASCD.

Tomlinson, C. A. (2010). *Leading and managing a differentiated classroom.* Alexandria, VA: ASCD.

Tomlinson, C. A., & Reis, S. M. (2004). *Differentiation for gifted and talented students.* Alexandria, VA: ASCD.

Van Note Chism, N., & Bickford, D. J. (2002). The importance of physical space in creating supportive learning environments. *New Directions for Teaching and Learning, Number 92.* San Francisco: Jossey-Bass.

Vander Ark, T. (2012). *Getting smart: How digital learning is changing the world.* San Francisco: Jossey-Bass.

Weber, Max. (1930/1958). *The Protestant ethic and the spirit of capitalism* (tr. Talcott Parsons). New York: Charles Scribner's Sons.

Index

The letter *f* following a page number denotes a figure.

Class Photo Book activity, 47–48
Collins, Jim, 58
consistency vs. speed of work, 58, 65
CRT (culturally responsive teaching), 69–70, 69*f*
cultural identities, 8
culturally responsive teaching (CRT), 69–70, 69*f*

data interpretation, 71–72
decision trees, 69–70, 69*f*
deferred gratification, 59–60, 66
dropout/graduation rates, 55
Duckworth, Angela, 63

entitlement, sense of, 48–49, 60
environment's effects on student learning
  comfortable seating, 15–16
  de-centeredness, 16
  flexible spaces, 15
  locker size and building layout, 12

research on, 11
sensory stimulation, 16
student input on design of physical spaces, 12–13, 17–18
students' ideas, receptiveness to, 14–15
and students' well-being, 13–14, 18
technology's role, 16
epiphanies, walking students into
  about friends, family, and community, 47–48
  about meaningful/successful work, 58, 60
  about patience and time, 48–50
  about plagiarism, 59
  classroom wall items to facilitate, 22, 22f, 24, 24f, 27–28
  cursing example, 21–23, 22*f*
  frog-in-the-well story, 25–26
  90/10 reaction/performance ratio, 24–25, 25*f*
  pick-up-your-pants example, 23–24, 24*f*

expertise in students, nurturing
  Class Photo Book activity, 47–48
  considering how famous people
    became experts, 48, 53
  faith in students' potential, 43–44, 70
  friendship activities, 47–48
  homework that's relevant to students'
    lives, 44–45
  identifying mentors and influencers,
    45–47, 52
  patience and time, 48–50
  practicing with purpose, 44–45, 52

friendships, developing, 47–48

Glasser, William, 20
graduation/dropout rates, 55
Great by Choice (Collins), 58

honesty, 58–59, 65

individual educational plans (IEPs), 31
Ingham, Harry, 3

Johari Window, 3–5, 4*f*

Luft, Joseph, 3

masks, 3
mentors and influencers, 45–47, 52
Minority-Majority Moments, 5–6
Motion Picture Association of America
    (MPAA) rating system, 21–23, 22*f*
motivation, 60
MPAA (Motion Picture Association of
    America) rating system, 21–23, 22*f*

90/10 reaction/performance ratio,
    24–25, 25*f*

NPEI (No-Punishment Empowerment
    Intervention)
  an application of, 32–34
  checklist, 35*f*
  intervention tool, 36–39*f*
  steps, 31

patience and time, 48–50
peer influence/pressure, 47, 50
Perry, Andre, 70
Photo Book activity, 47–48
plagiarism, 58–59
practicing with purpose, 44–45, 52
pride, 60
productive times/places for study, 50
Protestant work ethic, 57
punishment, alternatives to. *See* NPEI

race, assumptions about, 1–2, 6–7
reality therapy. *See also* epiphanies,
    walking students into; NPEI
  addressing chronically disruptive
    students, 30–31
  building a better relationship,
    29–30
  counseling, 30
  immediate actions as focus of, 20
  Rules of Engagement, 5

saying "no" to peer pressure, 50
self-awareness strategies
  re cultural identities, 8
  goals of, 8–9
  Johari Window, 3–5, 4*f*
  masks, 3
  Minority-Majority Moments, 5–6
  Rules of Engagement, 5
  self-awareness defined, 2

sleep, 50
Socratic method, 20–21
student assumptions about teachers, 1–2, 6–7
study times/places, 50

teachers
culturally responsive teaching (CRT) by, 69–70, 69f
engagement with the community, 71
faith in students' potential, 43–44, 70
proving student success, 71–72
seeking help from colleagues, 44, 70
self-aware, 67–68
student assumptions about, 1–2, 6–7

time management, 49–50
to-do lists, 49–50

Weber, Max, 57
work ethic
assessing, 62–63
consistency vs. speed, 58, 65
deferred gratification, 59–60, 66
graduation/dropout rates linked to, 55
honesty, emphasis on, 58–59, 65
meanings of, 56–57, 64
in the real world (post–high school), 55–56
satisfying vs. useful work, 57–58, 64
self-monitoring progress, 60–62

About the Author

Ignacio Lopez, EdD, is Vice Provost and Associate Professor of Education at National Louis University in Chicago. Dr. Lopez has presented and spoken at numerous national teacher conferences and school district events. He is a member of the ASCD cadre, and serves as a board member for School District 73 in Illinois.

Related ASCD Resources

At the time of publication, the following resources were available (ASCD stock numbers appear in parentheses):

Print Products

Educational Leadership: Culturally Diverse Classrooms (March 2015) (#115021)

Educating Everybody's Children: Diverse Teaching Strategies for Diverse Learners, Revised and Expanded 2nd Edition by Robert W. Cole (#107003)

Connecting Teachers, Students, and Standards by Debora L. Voltz, Michele Jean Sims, and Betty Nelson (#109011)

Managing Diverse Classrooms: How to Build on Students' Cultural Strengths by Carrie Rothstein-Fisch and Elise Trumbull (#107014)

For up-to-date information about ASCD resources, go to www.ascd.org. You can search the complete archives of Educational Leadership at www.ascd.org/el.

ASCD EDge® Group

Exchange ideas and connect with other educators on the social networking site ASCD EDge at http://ascdedge.ascd.org/.

ASCD myTeachSource®

Download resources from a professional learning platform with hundreds of research-based best practices and tools for your classroom at http://myteachsource.ascd.org/.

For more information, send an e-mail to member@ascd.org; call 1-800-933-2723 or 703-578-9600; send a fax to 703-575-5400; or write to Information Services, ASCD, 1703 N. Beauregard St., Alexandria, VA 22311-1714 USA.